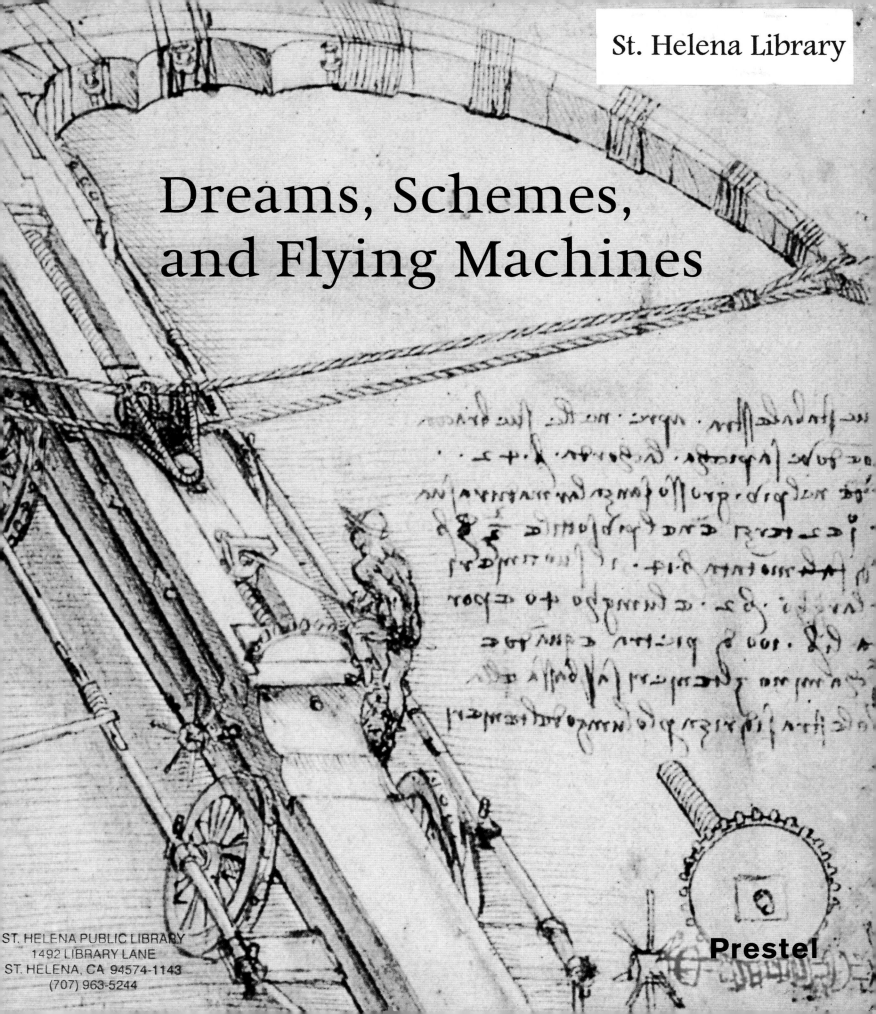

Dreams, Schemes, and Flying Machines

Prestel

"Of the Sky and of the Earth"

was to be the title of a large book on nature in which Leonardo da Vinci, an artist by profession who lived some 500 years ago, wanted to bring together the results of his studies. He never completed the book. But in his lifetime Leonardo recorded his ideas, experiments, and conclusions in countless drawings and sheets and sheets of notes.

For Leonardo the world was full of riddles and mysteries. And he was interested in all of them, wanting to know everything. He studied many things in nature and science. Still, many questions remained unanswered.

What makes the moon glow?

Leonardo realized that the moon itself has no light but simply reflects the light of the sun.

But how and why?

Is the moon made of crystal?

Is there water on the moon?

Perhaps, he thought, the moon's surface is covered in water and the sun's rays are reflected off of the moving waters on the moon. That might be why the moon shines!

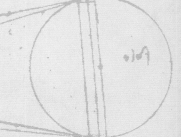

But why does the moon cast a shadow?

And why are the shaded areas of the moon still brighter than the dark night sky? Is sunlight reflected off the oceans on earth back onto the areas of water on the moon?

Why is the sky blue?

"The blueness we see in the sky is not really a colour," Leonardo wrote in his notebook. He discovered that warm vapours and minute atoms are captured in the sun's rays and these make the air appear blue against the black of the infinite space beyond.

Writing secrets

Leonardo had a secretive way of recording his discoveries: he made all his notes in mirror writing. First of all, this was a practical choice: Leonardo was left-handed and by writing in reverse, he avoided smudging the ink. Secondly, it gave him a little bit of secrecy. Because many of Leonardo's ideas and experiments were about things that were forbidden in his time.

3

The Mystery of Water

More than anything else, Leonardo was fascinated by water. Throughout his life he studied and worked with water time and time again.

He admired the beauty of whirlpools, of eddies and waves, of bubbles and drops, and the power that water has to uproot trees and even destroy houses. He was intrigued by the different bodies of water—the sea, rivers, and other watercourses, as well as things built for water, such as pipes, canals, dams, locks, bridges, or machines driven by its force. And of course, Leonardo loved anything and everything that moved on water.

Do bursting bubbles make a sound?

"Why," Leonardo asked himself, "can shells sometimes be found on mountain tops?" Some of his contemporaries thought that the Deluge, or the Flood described in the Bible, must have deposited them there. But Leonardo disagreed. He knew that the marine creatures that lived in the shells liked to stay near the ocean floor, not near the surface. Could it be, he wondered, that the seabed had gradually been lifted and when the Mediterranean waters poured out through the Strait of Gibraltar that shells had then been deposited on the top of mountains?

How did shells get to be on the top of a mountain?

Where do tides come from?

Are they somehow connected to the sun and the moon?

Where do rivers come from?

Perhaps their water comes
from underground watercourses
below the ocean floor?

And where does water flow to?

Leonardo carried out lots and lots of experiments.
"What happens when I place rocks into a stream," he thought?
"How can I direct which way water flows?"
"What creates a whirlpool?"

A waterfall, a jet of water—and then?

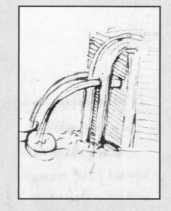

Studying the Human Body

How do our bodies work?

What makes an arm move?
How do muscles and tendons work?

How does breath flow?

How do our voices work?

Leonardo knew so much about the human body because he had a never-ending curiosity to study and search for answers. At that time dissecting a corpse was considered a crime and punishable by death. But Leonardo secretly cut open many corpses to study muscles, bones, joints, tendons, and organs. And he made hundreds of drawings on human anatomy.

These sketches show the skeleton of the torso, the lung and the windpipe, and the strands of muscles in the arm.

Unfortunately, the doctors who lived during Leonardo's time did not make use of his discoveries. But this was the first time in history that the human body became an object of scientific research.

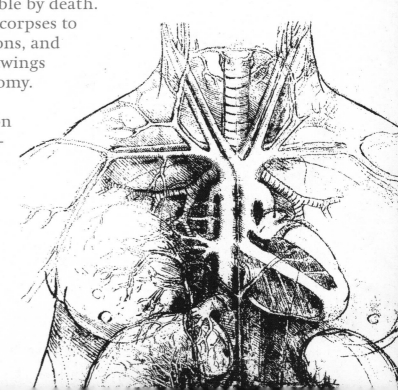

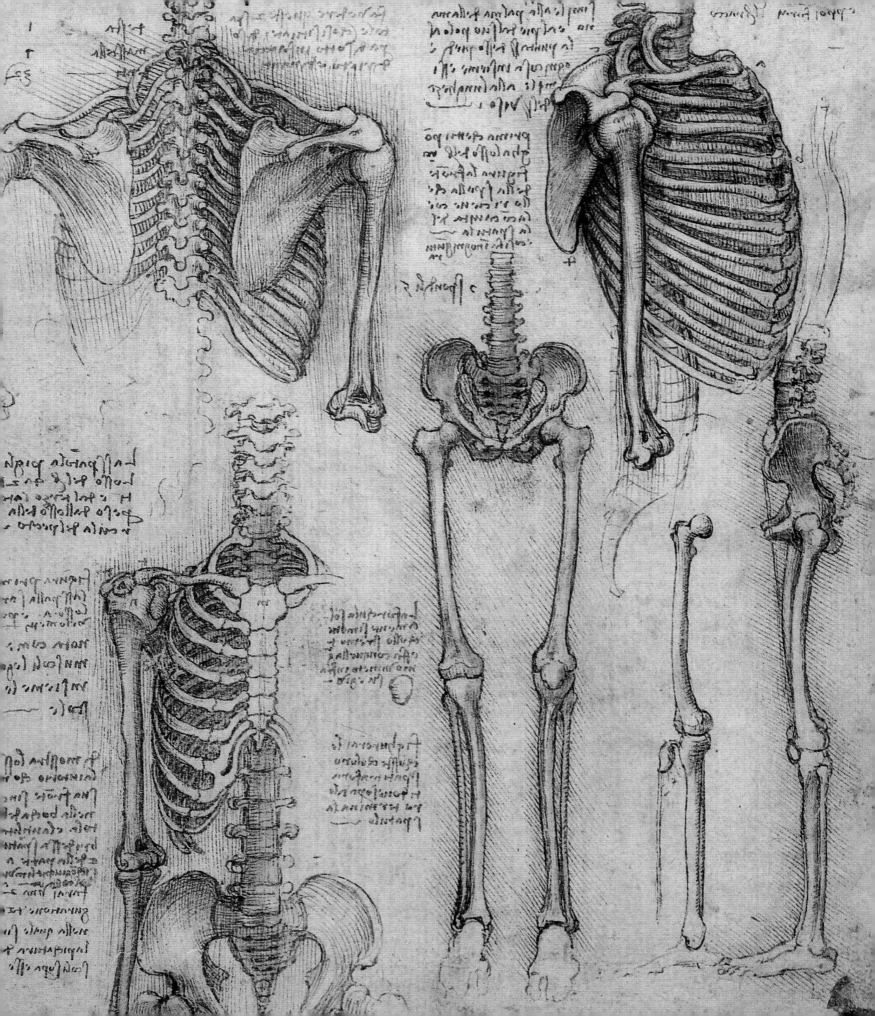

How does an unborn baby grow inside its mother?

From Leonardo's studies on animals he learned how a baby grows inside its mother. He drew detailed sketches and noted everything down: the function of the umbilical cord, the womb, and the liquid that surrounds and protects a growing baby, as well as how organs develop.

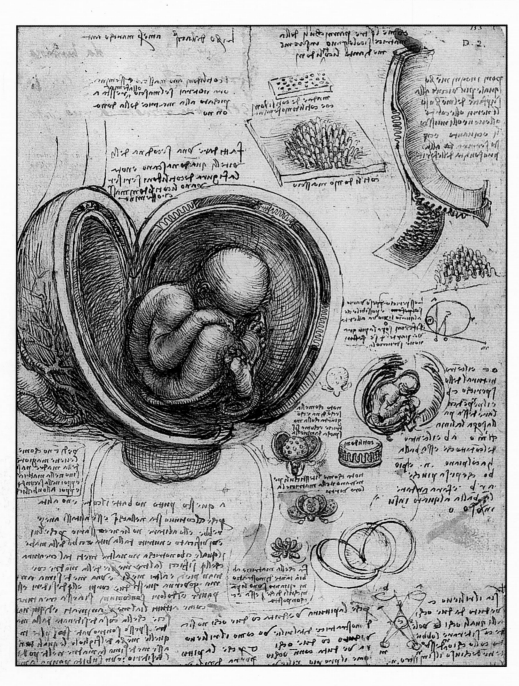

Leonardo studied the proportions of the human body. To his eyes, the human body was the measure of all things. He tried to look at it in terms of geometry: how large is a head in proportion to the rest of the body? How long should arms and legs be?

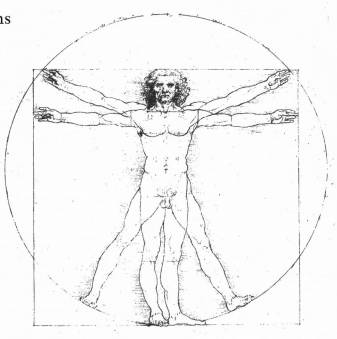

How have we been put together?

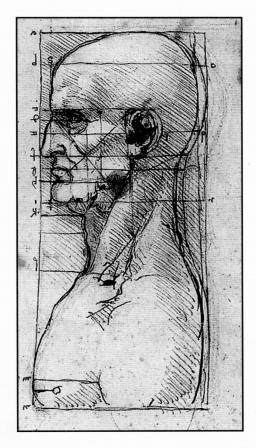

How long should a nose be?

Next to this drawing of a head in profile, Leonardo jotted down notes on proportion: the full length of a body, he calculated, is eight times that of the head.

Leonardo divided human physical features into different categories. This is what he had to say about noses: "Of noses there are nine varieties: straight, crooked, bent, those which are prominent above the middle point, and those which are so below the middle, hawk noses, stub noses, round noses, and pointed noses."

And then there are faces that defy description. So Leonardo drew them instead and here are some of his sketches of fascinating facial features.

The Dream of Flying

How do birds fly?

This question fascinated Leonardo all his
life. Again and again he would sketch a bird
in flight. As he sat drawing, many questions
came into his head:
How are bird wings constructed?
How do birds glide?
How can birds steer?
How can birds fly against the wind?
And, of course: how do birds land?

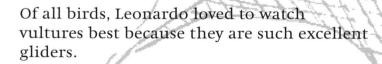

Of all birds, Leonardo loved to watch
vultures best because they are such excellent
gliders.

His studies on the flight of birds were the
basis for the invention of a flying machine
intended to help humans conquer the skies.

These drawings are of a wing and a flying
machine to be driven by muscle power using
a special mechanism.

A few years ago a model was built using
Leonardo's plans for a flying machine. This
image shows how the pilot is supposed to
hang beneath the body of the machine.

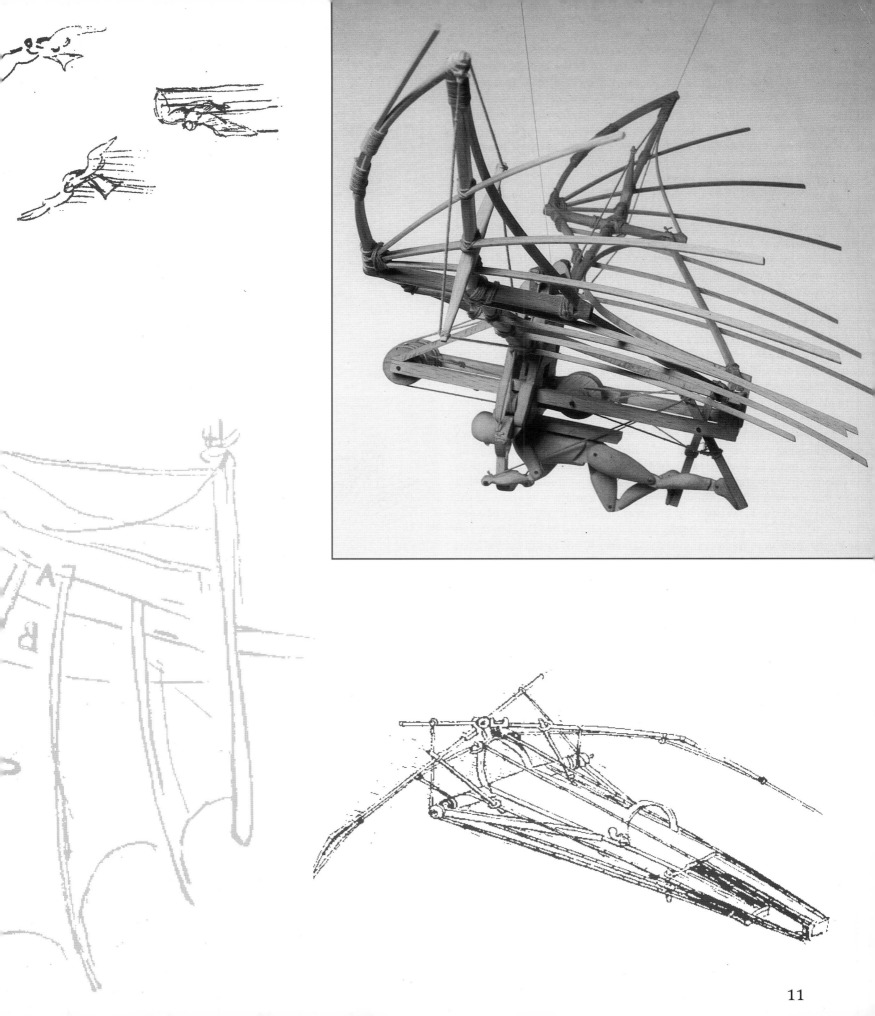

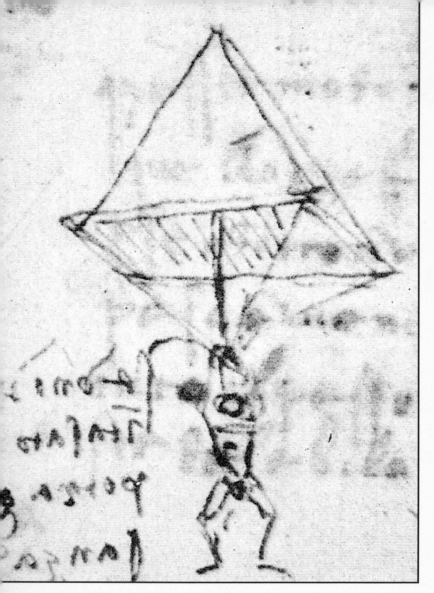

Can the wind carry a person?

"If a person were to have a tent made of fabric ten yards long and just as wide, he could fall from any height without injury."

There was the answer ... and Leonardo had just invented the parachute!

How do helicopters rise into the air?

Leonardo also invented a kind of helicopter. He called it an "airscrew." Leonardo was quite sure that if the "airscrew" were made to turn round very fast indeed it would lift off into the air. He never constructed one to put his theory to the test but he was right after all. Modern airplane propellers and helicopters are based on the same principle.

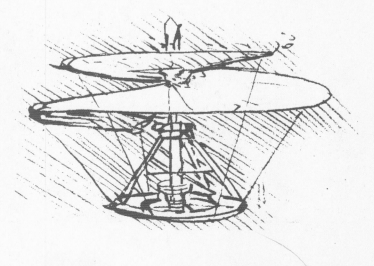

How do biplanes land?

The biplane with mobile wings is reminiscent of the early airplanes of the twentieth century. The ladders for climbing into the flying machine are an interesting feature. They were also intended to absorb the shock upon landing. In flight, the ladders were to be pulled up into the plane, much like the retractable landing gear on modern aircraft.

The biplane was to be driven by muscle power. The pilot was supposed to push a rod with his head, simultaneously turn knobs with both hands and press down on a footboard with his body weight. If you think this sounds a bit complicated, you're right! But simplicity was never Leonardo's cup of tea.

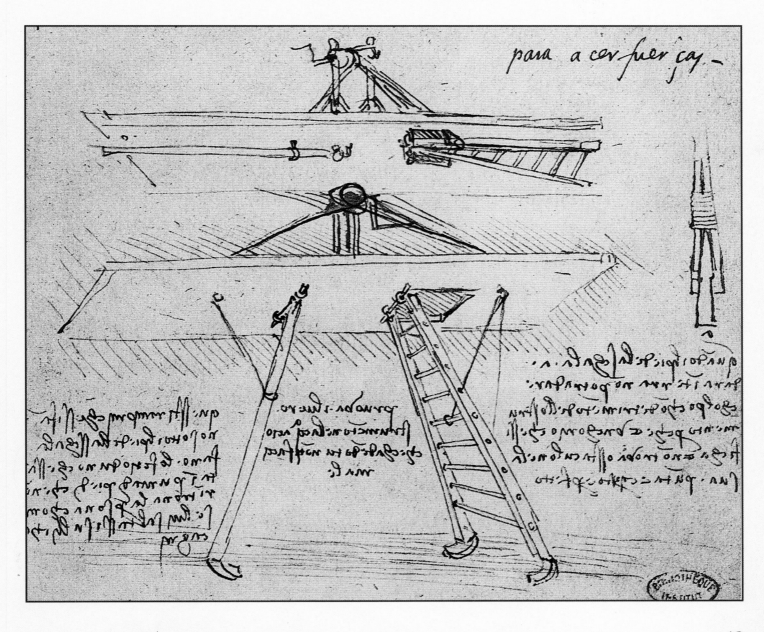

The Automobile

Leonardo invented an amazing number of
things that were re-invented again hundreds
of years later.

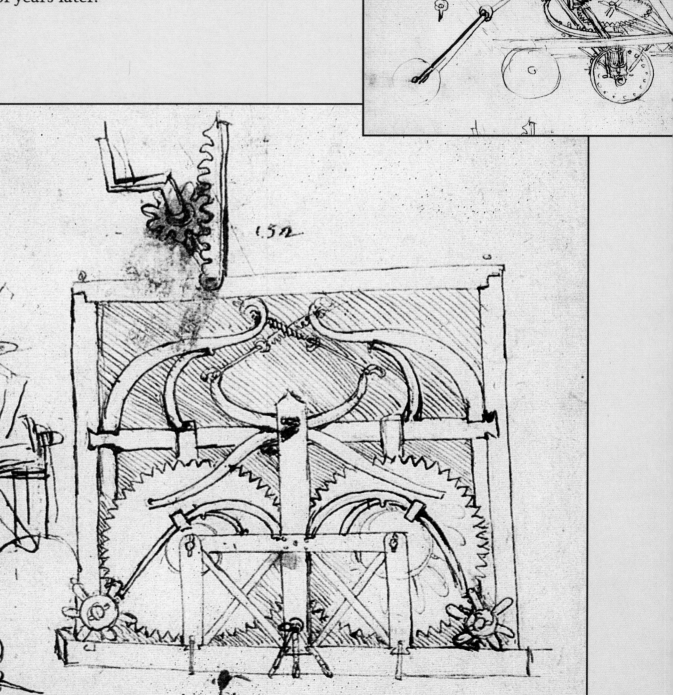

How to drive a cart without a horse?

Leonardo dreamt of machines made for transportation—on water, in the air, or across land. One of his inventions was an "automobile." Leonardo's automobile can really be considered the forerunner of the modern car.

The "motor" consisted of a system of springs. Just like a toycar it had to be constantly rewound. Leonardo never built his "automobile," but had he done so, he would have found it very tiring to drive.

Many of Leonardo's inventions existed only as sketches: the pivoting bridge, for example, and crankshafts and gears, or a water-operated alarm clock. In the end, Leonardo was known as the man who never finished what he had begun. But he was happy to identify a problem and then solve it, even if it was only in theory.

On Lifting and Pushing

How can heavy loads be shifted?

Simple: with cranes and levers.
This solution was very significant for work on construction sites.

This sketch of a "lifting machine" shows a rope fed across two pulleys (at the top) which leads down to a winch below. With the help of the cog wheel and the threads running up the central pole, even heavy weights can be lifted easily. The whole apparatus also rotates which makes it easier to pick up loads (such as bricks) from different angles.

Why is it easier to push things on bearings or wheels?

Easy: because they are round and only a small part of their surface touches the ground.

The lifting machine designed to erect columns has a screw thread. To make turning the wheel easier, Leonardo placed the nut on top of a wheel bearing.

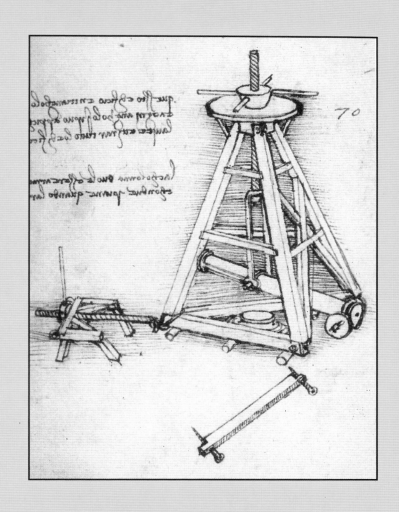

What's so great about long levers?

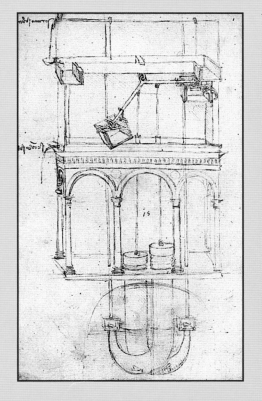

A simple law of physics: the longer the lever, the less power is needed. People knew about this law even in Leonardo's time. And Leonardo applied this knowledge to his mechanical inventions.

This pump installation with levers works much like the mechanism inside the water tank in every toilet. The water pump is controlled by two floaters. When water is let out (Leonardo drew a stream of water flowing out of the pump on the left-hand side of the drawing), the pump automatically draws in more water until the floater rises to the top again.

The Painter

Leonardo da Vinci painted what is probably the most famous picture in the world. It is called *Mona Lisa* and you can see it in a museum in Paris, the Louvre.

Who was Mona Lisa?

The Mona Lisa's real name was probably Lisa Gherardini. At the age of sixteen she married a wealthy merchant called Francesco del Giocondo who was some twenty years older. That was in Florence in 1495. It was a very happy marriage and Francesco del Giocondo commissioned Leonardo to paint a portrait of his beloved wife.

But the painting is full of mystery ....

Why did Franceso del Giocondo never receive the picture?

Because Leonardo never gave away the painting of the woman with the mysterious smile but kept it by his side until his death many years later.

The painting technique of a genius

In several paintings Leonardo used a new technique called "Sfumato". "Sfumato" is Italian for "smoky." In painting, this means using muted colours and soft contours that seem to dissolve. This makes the image in the painting look as if it were surrounded by a gentle mist.

How do you paint directly on a wall?

Leonardo's fresco, or wall painting, *The Last Supper* is almost as famous as his *Mona Lisa*. He used a technique of his own invention which enabled him to brush paint directly onto the wall in the refectory—or dining hall—of the Santa Maria delle Grazie monastery in Milan. When he had finished, the colours were beautiful and luminous. But they didn't last long. After a few years the paint began to flake off and the huge wall painting became badly damaged. People have tried several times to restore and rescue the painting, but the damp walls make it extremely difficult. Only recently has an extensive, year-long restoration been successfully completed.

What's happening in the picture?

The painting shows Jesus and the Disciples at the Last Supper. Jesus has just told them that one of them is going to betray him. And now pandemonium has broken out. The twelve apostles are talking in a very lively way. Only Jesus sits quietly in the middle.

Where is the traitor Judas?

Judas is among the group of three disciples to the left of Jesus. He has pulled back in fear and is looking at Jesus with wide eyes. In his right hand he clutches the purse that contains thirty silver pieces—the reward for his betrayal.

How War Put an End to a Monument

Leonardo had been commissioned by the Duke of Milan, Ludovico Sforza, to create a bronze rider's monument for Ludovico's father, Franceso Sforza. The artist made many sketches of horses and of monuments, gathered information about bronze casting and finally completed a clay model of the monument. When the project was ready to be carried out—after nearly ten years of preparation—French troops marched into Milan and put an end to the project's successful completion. Bronze was needed to make more cannon balls and the French army destroyed the impressive clay model of the rider on a horse.

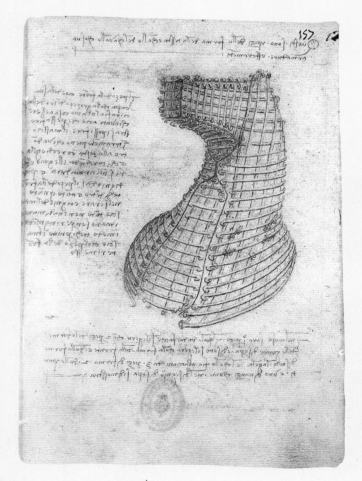

How to cast a horse in bronze?

First you have to make a hollow mold into which the liquid bronze is poured. The drawing on the left shows how Leonardo envisioned the outer construction of the hollow form for the horse's head. Because liquid bronze exerts a huge amount of pressure on the form, Leonardo had planned to attach a number of metal rods to make it stronger.

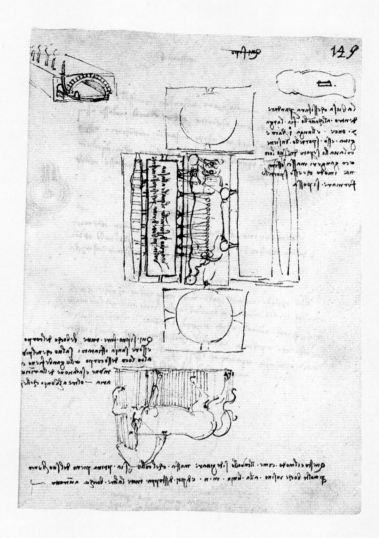

The drawing on the right illustrates the process of pouring bronze. The hollow form of the horse's head has been hung upside down. Bronze would then be poured into the form through the many holes on the bottom. This would have had to be done very carefully to prevent air bubbles from forming which would have destroyed the fine outlines of the sculpture.

What would Leonardo's bronze horse have looked like?

500 years later, an American admirer of Leonardo's work arranged for the statue to be cast using the Renaissance artist's original plans. The bronze horse, measuring more than seven metres high and weighing some fifteen tonnes, was completed in 1999 exactly according to Leonardo's drawings, and was then presented to the city of Milan.

Times of War

Leonardo lived at a time when wars were frequent. One of his most important tasks was to invent new weapons for his patrons.

One of his inventions was this precursor to the machine gun, a shotgun with multiple barrels which meant that it wasn't necessary to reload it after each shot.

Another remarkable invention was Leonardo's design for a giant crossbow which had an impressive range and yet could still be operated by just one man.

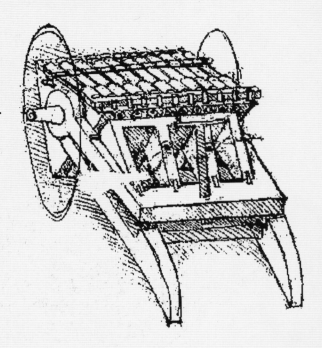

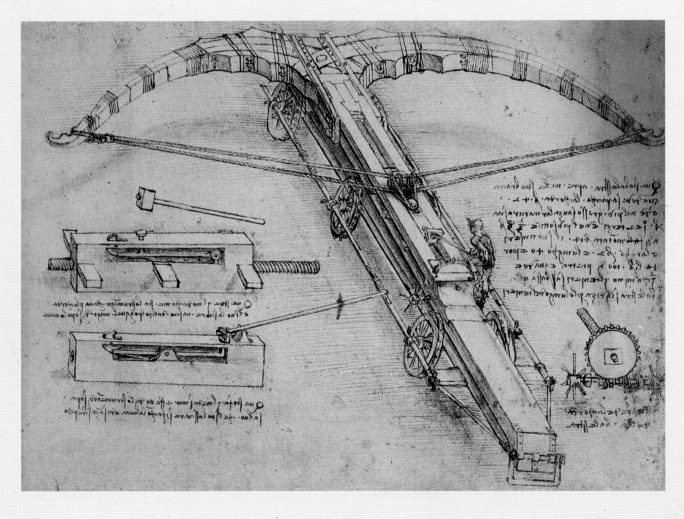

What is the best way to fend off enemies?

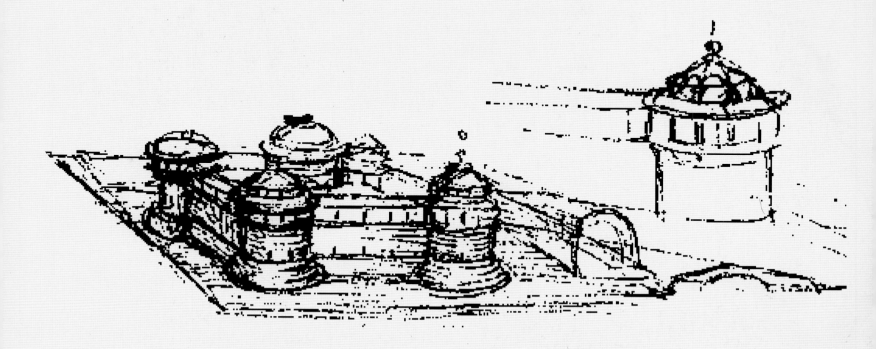

For defense purposes, Leonardo designed city walls, towers, and fortified structures.

One of his most curious ideas was a plan for a movable dam. Leonardo thought that the movable dam could be used to flood areas and drown enemies.

One of Leonardo's most interesting ideas was an armored vehicle made of wood which was to be pushed forward by the soldiers inside it. This meant that horses would no longer have been needed—a much welcomed development as they were such easy targets in battles.

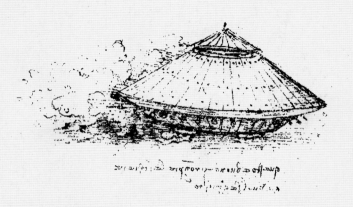

Leonardo's weapons, his defense installations, and the armored car were never built. Today, some of the objects in his plans have been constructed just as he designed them. The amazing thing is that the machines really do work!

The Renaissance

The period during which Leonardo lived is called the Renaissance. It was a time of great innovation and change in politics, religion, and culture. It began in Italy and spread across the whole of central Europe.

Literally translated, Renaissance means "rebirth" and it refers to the rebirth of traditions from Antiquity. The Renaissance was a time when knowledge and education were prized above all, coupled with a great enthusiasm for the antique art of the Ancient Greeks. The Renaissance was also the time when people began to really understand the world around them: they studied space, time, shape, and proportion. Perspective, too, was studied and perfected during the Renaissance.

The "Uomo universale" was the ideal of the time: a "Universal Man," or as we still say "a Renaissance man," is someone who knows everything, can do everything and can be everything. No one embodies this ideal better than Leonardo with his insatiable curiosity and his thirst for knowledge.

Leonardo da Vinci was a multi-talented genius. He was a painter, but he was also an inventor, a researcher, a scientist, an architect, and an engineer. He was highly intelligent and an extremely astute observer of nature.

Leonardo's *Self-Portrait* at the age of 62.

Leonardo was born on April 15, 1452 in a small village near Vinci in northern Italy. Leonardo da Vinci simply means: Leonardo from Vinci.

When he was around seventeen years old he moved to Florence with his father Pietro, an established notary. Florence was about 40 km from Vinci and at that time it was a famous centre of culture: many renowned artists lived there. Leonardo became an apprentice to Andrea del Verrocchio, a painter, sculptor, and goldsmith. By the time he was twenty, Leonardo could paint as well as his teacher.

Leonardo—A Life full of Activity

Leonardo stayed in Florence for a few more years, first as the head of Verrocchio's painting studio and then as an independent artist.

When he turned thirty, he moved to Milan to enter into the service of its ruling family, the Sforza. Leonardo also designed stage sets and even participated in directing plays. When the Sforza were overthrown in 1499, Leonardo returned to Florence where he worked as a geographer, an anatomist, and a painter.

In 1507 the versatile artist and natural scientist was called back to Milan—this time by Charles d'Amboise, governor for the King of France. In the years that followed, Leonardo had to write many expert reports on building projects for his patron. Otherwise he could pursue his many interests and study and work as he pleased because his highest patron, King Louis XII of France, gave him a free reign.

Nevertheless, in 1513 Leonardo decided to try his luck in Rome. But his hopes for good commissions from the Pope were never fulfilled. The Pope was already employing three other Renaissance masters: Michelangelo, a painter and sculptor; Raphael, a painter; and Bramante, a master architect.

When Louis XII died, François I ascended the throne. This king also appreciated the genius of Leonardo, who was growing old. At the end of 1516 he invited the master to go to France and gave him a small castle called Cloux near Amboise as his home. And in this manner Leonardo spent the last years of his life as advisor to King François I of France, although this period was not a very productive one for Leonardo.

Leonardo da Vinci died on May 2, 1519.

Leonardo da Vinci's works can now be found in museums and collections all over the world.

In Vinci, near Florence in Italy, the Museo Leonardiano is devoted to the town's famous son and displays many machines and models of Leonardo's inventions. A few miles away in Anchiano, the house where the artist was born can also be visited.

The illustrations in this book:

Leonardo's manuscripts (MS) are sorted by letter, e.g. MS A, B, C, etc. Others are in the form of handwritten books known as codices:
The **Codex Leicester** is privately owned by Melinda and Bill Gates;
The so-called **Codex Atlanticus** is in the collection of the Biblioteca Ambrosiana in Milan;
The **Codex 8936** written by Leonardo is registered in the Biblioteca National in Madrid under that number.

Front cover:
Model of Leonardo's flying machine (see page 11);
Self-Portrait (see page 26)

Title page:
Design for a giant crossbow (detail), Codex Atlanticus
(see page 24)

pages 2/3:
Drawings of the sun, moon and the earth
Codex Leicester

page 4:
Waves, Codex Leicester;
Dredger, MS E, Institut de France, Paris

page 5:
Effect caused by obstacles on the movements of flowing water, Codex Leicester;
Redirecting a watercourse, Codex Leicester;
Effect of jets of water on a waterfall, Codex Leicester;
Water hose, Codex Leicester;
An experiment to raise the water level, Codex Leicester

page 6:
Arm muscle, anatomy sketchbooks, vol. A., Royal Collection, Windsor Castle;
Organs in the chest cavity, anatomy sketchbooks, vol. I., Royal Collection, Windsor Castle

page 7:
Anatomical studies of the human skeleton, Royal Collection, Windsor Castle

page 8:
Human foetus in open womb, anatomy sketchbooks, vol. III., Royal Collection, Windsor Castle

page 9:
Canon of proportions (Vitruvian Man), Galeria dell'Accademia, Venice;
Bust of man in profile, Galleria dell' Accademia, Venice;
Grotesque faces, Royal Collection, Windsor Castle

pages 10/11:
Studies of birds in flight, Biblioteca Reale, Turin;
Plan of a ribbed wing, partially covered in taffeta, MS B, Institut de France, Paris;
Fuselage of a flying machine, MS B, Institut de France, Paris;
Model of an airplane constructed in the twentieth century based on Leonardo's original drawings

page 12:
Parachute, Codex Atlanticus;
Airscrew, MS B, Institut de France, Paris

page 13:
Airplane with landing ladders, MS D, Institut de France, Paris

page 14:
Section and draft for a self-propelling vehicle, Codex Atlanticus

page 15:
Model of an "automobile," twentieth-century construction based on a sketch by Leonardo

page 16:
Design for a machine to lift heavy objects, Codex Atlanticus

page 17:
Design for a machine to erect columns, Codex Atlanticus;
Design for a hydraulic machine, Codex Atlanticus

page 19:
Mona Lisa, oil on wood, 77 x 53 cm, Louvre, Paris

pages 20/21:
The Last Supper, oil and mixed tempera on plaster, 420 x 910 cm, refectory at Santa Maria delle Grazie, Milan
Photo: Elemond, Electa Archive

page 22:
Drawing for an equestrian monument for Francesco Sforza, Royal Collection, Windsor Castle;
Studies for the casting form for the horse's head and neck, Codex 8936

page 23:
Studies for casting the horse, Codex 8936;
Bronze horse cast using Leonardo's plans, 1999. The horse is a gift to the Italian people from the people of America. This illustration shows the completed 24-foot bronze horse on view in America before being disassembled and shipped to Milan, Italy.
Photo: Walter Garschagen.
Reproduced by kind permission of Leonardo da Vinci's Horse Inc., Pennsylvania

page 24:
Design for multibarrel shotgun, Codex Atlanticus;
Design for a giant crossbow, Codex Atlanticus

page 25:
Draft for a fortress, Codex Atlanticus;
Sketch for an armored vehicle, The British Museum, London

page 26:
Self-portrait, circa 1516, red chalk drawing, Biblioteca Reale, Turin

page 29:
A dragon among cats (detail), Royal Collection, Windsor Castle

Back cover: Cat (detail), Royal Collection, Windsor Castle